MORMONS

How to Respond
Updated Edition

Edgar P. Kaiser

A CHRISTIAN WITNESS

CONCORDIA PUBLISHING HOUSE · SAINT LOUIS

This edition published 2010 Concordia Publishing House.
Text copyright © 1977, 1995 Concordia Publishing House.
3558 S. Jefferson Avenue, St. Louis, MO 63118-3968
1-800-325-3040 • www.cph.org

Originally published as *How to Respond to the Latter Day Saints* in The Response Series © 1977 Concordia Publishing House.

Manufactured in the United States of America

Library of Congress Cataloging-in-Publication Data
Kaiser, Edgar P.
    The Latter-day Saints / Edgar P. Kaiser. —Rev. ed.
       p.   cm.   —(How to respond series)
    Rev. ed. of: How to respond to—The Latter-day Saints. © 1977.
    Includes bibliographical references and index.
    ISBN 0-7586-1624-4
1. Church of Jesus Christ of Latter-day Saints—Controversial literature. 2. Mormon Church—Controversial literature. I. Kaiser, Edgar P. How to respond to—the Latter-day Saints. II. Title. III. Series.
BX8645.K28 1995
230'.93—dc20   95–22606

1 2 3 4 5 6 7 8 9 10   19 18 17 16 15 14 13 12 11 10

CONTENTS

1 FROM PALMYRA TO PARADISE

You've seen the young men dressed in white shirts and ties, a stark contrast with what most young men wear today. They walk down the street or ride bicycles. If you engage them in conversation on a street corner or at your door, you will find them to be well mannered and courteous. You recognize them as Mormon missionaries.

They seem to be everywhere. You can find them throughout the United States and in many countries around the world. A feature article in *U.S. News & World Report* stated:

> Today The Church of Jesus Christ of Latter-day Saints, better known as the Mormon Church, is one of the world's richest and fastest-growing religious movements. Since World War II, its ranks have quadrupled to more than 8.3 million members worldwide with 4.5 million U.S. members. . . . What ultimately attracts new converts to Mormonism, Mormon leaders and religion

experts outside the church agree, is distinctive teachings that, on the one hand, seem comfortingly familiar to people of Christian background but that often go dramatically beyond the tenets of traditional Christianity.[1]

Who are these "Mormons," as they are popularly known? What do they believe? How did their "distinctive" yet "comfortingly familiar" beliefs and their organization come to be?

THE RELIGIOUS CLIMATE

The history of the Church of Jesus Christ of Latter-day Saints (LDS) takes us back to the early 1800s. The name "Mormon" is a nickname that has become widely adopted to refer to the LDS; it comes from the prophet Mormon, who supposedly wrote the chief scriptures of the Latter-day Saints, the Book of Mormon. The spiritual revival that began in the mid-1700s under the leadership of Jonathan Edwards and others had died down. The spiritual condition of people in the United States was at a low ebb. Then in the early 1800s came the Second Great Awakening. This revival, centered around the "camp meeting," tended to stress emotional responses. Those who became fired up gave special attention to spreading the revival to western New York State. Evangelization of this area of the newly formed United States of America was so intense it became known as the "Burned-over District." One evangelist after another visited it, and revivals were held almost continually in one community or another throughout the area.

Charles Finney had set the country aflame with his so-called "New Measures" and his dramatic revival methods. In addition, Alexander Campbell (Disciples of Christ), Jemima Wilkinson (or Wilkerson—the Shakers), and many others were active evangelists at this time. They emphasized what a human being could accomplish to bring about eternal salvation for one's self.[2]

JOSEPH SMITH JR.

In this religious climate of fervent evangelistic activity, Joseph Smith Jr. grew up near Palmyra, New York. He was born in Vermont on December 23, 1805. Around the age of eleven he moved with his family to Manchester, New York. The Smiths were of solid Yankee stock. Joseph's maternal ancestors, the Macks, were of Scotch Dissenter stock. Both families had lived in New England since the 1600s.

Joseph seems to have been an agreeable and likable young man. He was intelligent and loved adventure.

Some, though, considered him an idle young man who spent his days digging for buried treasure. Since treasure hunters were often impacted by "evil influences," Joseph used a "peepstone"—an egg-shaped stone he had found—supposedly to locate the treasures. Such "innocent" occultism seems to have occupied much of the life of the young Joseph Smith Jr.

As a teenager, Joseph could hardly have escaped exposure to the religious fervor of the times. By his own account, he was much disturbed by the religious confusion of his day. Which of the many evangelists was correct? Accepting literally the words of the letter of James in the New Testament, Joseph went into the woods to ask God for wisdom. He claims that God the Father and His Son appeared to him there. They advised Joseph not to join any of the religious groups active at the time, for their creeds were all an abomination before the Lord. Instead, he was told to await further word. According to the official version published by the Mormon Church, Joseph was fourteen when he received this vision in the spring of 1820.

THE GOLDEN PLATES

8   Smith then claimed he received a series of revelations beginning in 1823 in which he was visited by the angel

Moroni. He told Joseph about some golden plates hidden on a little hill near Palmyra (now called Hill Cumorah). These plates, written by Moroni's father, the prophet Mormon, contained important writings, but Joseph was forbidden to remove these plates at that time. He was also told of a "magical" means for translating the writings on the plates. After four years of temptations and trial, the angel Moroni appeared to Joseph again and this time allowed him to take the plates.

Moroni's instructions to remove the plates from their hiding place in Hill Cumorah came in 1827, after Joseph had married Emma Hale. On September 22, 1827, the translation of the writings on the plates began. Many difficulties were endured before the translation was finished in June 1829. This translated document became the Book of Mormon.

Many difficulties were also encountered in printing the book. Some printers wanted cash. One prospective printer was threatened by Joseph's enemies. Finally, a friend, Martin Harris, sold part of his farm to get some cash so the printing could begin. (Chapter 5 will provide more details regarding the translation and contents of the Book of Mormon.)

In 1830, the Book of Mormon was finally published. Smith claimed it was a new revelation to meet the demands of a changing society. Here was a final word from God to end the religious confusion of the day.

A CHURCH FOUNDED

Two other important events took place during the translation of the golden plates. In May 1829, Joseph Smith and a companion, Oliver Cowdery, claimed they received the *Aaronic* priesthood from John the Baptist. Later these same two men said that Peter, James, and John visited them and gave to them the *Melchizedek* priesthood. The official power of the Church of Jesus Christ of Latter-day Saints rests in these two priesthoods.

By the time the Book of Mormon was published, Joseph Smith had gathered a small number of followers. The time had come for the formal incorporation of the new church. The Book of Mormon and the two priesthoods formed the foundation for the new organization. Joseph Smith Jr. was named "seer, translator, prophet, and apostle of Jesus Christ, an elder of the church." He was ordained by Oliver Cowdery. Oliver Cowdery was ordained an "elder unto this church of Christ." The other men present were received into membership by the laying on of hands. The Church of Jesus Christ of Latter-day Saints came into being on April 6, 1830, at the home of Peter Whitmer Sr., in Fayette, New York.

PERSECUTION BEGINS

The road for the new church was not easy. Many folks in the community remembered Joseph's past. Some believed him to be nothing more than a fraud and a blasphemer. Many of the new church's religious activities were challenged. Various misfortunes fell on members of the Smith family. The harassment the group experienced frightened Joseph's wife, Emma. At first she refused to officially join the new church. She urged Joseph to return to farming, since it offered security for their marriage. Several weeks passed before Emma finally joined her husband's church. She did so only after Joseph informed her of the following "revelation" he received in answer to her concerns:

Hearken unto the voice of the Lord your God, while I speak unto you, Emma Smith, my daughter. . . . Murmur not because of the things which thou hast not seen. . . . And the office of thy calling shall be for a comfort unto my servant, Joseph Smith, junior, thy husband. . . . And thou needest not fear, for thy husband shall support thee from the church. . . . Continue in the spirit of meekness

11

and beware of pride. Let thy soul delight in thy husband, and the glory which shall come upon him. Keep my commandments continually, and a crown of righteousness thou shalt receive. And except thou do this, where I am you cannot come.[3]

A significant event now took place in the history of the new church. Oliver Cowdery and three other men were sent on a mission to convert American Indians. In Ohio they met Sidney Rigdon, a Campbellite revivalist. In less than three weeks, Rigdon and his entire communal colony in Kirtland, Ohio, were baptized by the Mormon missionaries. Steeped in the piety of the Campbellites, Rigdon brought education and theological background into the Mormon group and contributed to its theological development.

"Mormonism, as it is called, must stand or fall on the story of Joseph Smith. He was either a prophet of God, divinely called, properly appointed and commissioned, or he was one of the biggest frauds this world has ever seen. There is no middle ground."

(Joseph Fielding Smith, *Doctrines of Salvation* [Salt Lake City: Bookcraft, 1954], 1:188)

THE EASTERN BOUNDARY OF THE PROMISED LAND

Sidney Rigdon convinced Joseph Smith to move his band of sixty followers to Kirtland, Ohio, three hundred miles west of Fayette. With 150 converts from the Campbellites already in Kirtland, the new colony now numbered over two hundred. They called Kirtland "the eastern boundary of the Promised Land."

The church began to take shape, with much importance placed on the Aaronic priesthood. A group of men known as "the twelve apostles" was chosen. People came from miles around to see this new religious community, and many were converted and stayed. The United Order of Enoch was established, through which private property became church property and private profit became church profit. This gave church leaders economic power. To help solidify the community, a temple was built. It was dedicated in 1836.

From Kirtland missionaries were sent out even farther west. Some of the missionaries gave glowing reports of Independence, Missouri, where, according to a revelation given to Joseph Smith, the New Jerusalem was to be built (*Doctrine and Covenants* 57:1–5). A settlement was established there, but persecution soon forced the new settlers to leave and form a new community in Ray County, Missouri, with Far West as the county seat.

Meanwhile, many problems arose in Kirtland. Amid whisperings about polygamous unions, some church leaders and others left the church. Economic disaster threatened when the Mormon bank failed. To calm things down, Joseph sent some of his best elders on a mission to England, while he left for a missionary tour into Canada.

Peace, however, did not come to Kirtland. Bitter fighting continued, and the church split. Together with Sidney Rigdon, Joseph fled Kirtland in the night and never returned. He headed for Far West and hoped for better days. Eventually most of the Saints left Kirtland and moved west.

NAUVOO

Unfortunately for Joseph and his followers, peace did not last long in Far West either. On election day, August 6, 1838, the attempt by non-Mormons to prevent Mormons from voting resulted in a riot. In the midst of the turmoil Joseph Smith was taken prisoner. He was sentenced by a court martial to be shot, but the troop commander refused to carry out the order. Joseph's life was spared.

The eight thousand saints now turned back east. They crossed the Mississippi River and purchased property fifty miles north of Quincy, Illinois. Here they built a new city Joseph named "Nauvoo," a name that he told his followers meant "a beautiful plantation" in Hebrew. Joseph laid out the town according to the plan he had used in Kirtland and Far West. A special lot was reserved for construction of a temple.

Life in Nauvoo was difficult. Many followers died that first year, but within a few years an imposing city stood on the site of the former swamp. The newcomers were welcomed by the citizens of Illinois. An amazing charter was granted the city. It established Nauvoo as an almost independent city-state. The community had its own military organization and could make and enforce its own laws.

Three major theological developments took place during the Nauvoo years: new definitions of God and man; new rituals; and new teachings regarding family relations that served as the basis for polygamous marriage. The latter caused the death of Joseph Smith.

Despite official denials, there is evidence that polygamous marriage was sanctioned and practiced for some time by Mormon leaders in Nauvoo.

15

Two excommunicated contractors attempted to expose the practice of polygamy. They published only one issue of a newspaper, the *Nauvoo Expositor,* before the city council approved the destruction of the press. The injured owners charged Joseph Smith with rioting and violating their civil rights.

MARTYRDOM

Governor Ford gave Joseph a promise of safe conduct if he would come peaceably to Carthage, Illinois, to face the riot charges against him. The prophet, his brother, Hyrum Smith, and several others made the trip—and were jailed there.

The Carthage militia was in charge of guarding the incarcerated Mormons. While in an upstairs cell, the four Mormon leaders were attacked by members of another local militia. In the ensuing gun battle on June 27, 1844, Joseph and Hyrum Smith were killed.

Fourteen years after he had founded his church and before his thirty-ninth birthday, the Mormon prophet gave his life in the struggle that his religious innovations had caused between his followers and their neighbors. To his adherents his brutal murder and his exemplary bravery in the face of it only proved his genuineness. . . . To the heroism and suffering, the effort and accomplishments, of the Mormon group was added a new and more precious sacrifice. The immediate practical effect would be disorganization, but the long-range effect of martyr's blood would be to strengthen the people whose cause he led.[4]

WAR ONCE MORE

The Saints did not react in vengeance, and the anti-Mormons did not press their "victory." As the Mormons struggled to replace their lost prophet, several divisions occurred within the church. Sidney Rigdon claimed to be the successor of Joseph Smith. However, he was rejected and went to Pennsylvania where he started a church of his own. The Smith family claimed that leadership of the church must remain in the family. They divided from the main body and formed what today is known as the Reorganized Church of Jesus Christ of Latter-day Saints. Other groups broke off under the leadership of men like James J. Strang, Martin Harris, and Alpheus Cutter. Eventually the affairs of the church would be placed in the hands of "the twelve apostles," with Brigham Young as president.

17

Soon those left in Nauvoo faced persecution again. Open conflict at times erupted. Although the temple was dedicated in Nauvoo in May 1845, the bulk of the Mormon population began to leave soon after. Eventually a group of French Utopian socialists inhabited the city. The temple, partially burned, was further destroyed by a tornado in 1850.

PARADISE AT LAST!

Many of the former Nauvoo residents straggled across Iowa and set up quarters on the present site of Omaha, Nebraska. They spent the winter of 1846 there. The next spring an advance party, led by Brigham Young, began the march to the Great Salt Basin of Utah.

After a journey of 102 days they reached the "Promised Land." During the next months, thousands of Mormon immigrants flowed into the valley. A civilization was established on the banks of the Great Salt Lake, Brigham Young was declared president, and a new era in the history of Mormonism began.

Under the leadership of Young the settlement grew and prospered. Mormons spread out into neighboring territories. These beginnings were the birth pangs of a genuinely "American" church body: the Church of Jesus Christ of Latter-day Saints.

2 GOD OR GODS?

When considering the main teachings of the Church of Jesus Christ of Latter-day Saints, a logical place to start is with their teaching about God.

THE TRINITY

Mormon theology uses the word *Trinity* in speaking of God; and Father, Son, and Holy Spirit are indeed meant. The Mormons baptize in the name of this "Trinity." However, in Mormon teaching, the Father, the Son, and the Holy Spirit each are a distinct god. These are three entities or beings—three gods (though in terms of greatness, the Father is first, Jesus is second, and the Holy Spirit is third). In Mormonism, the oneness of the Trinity is not found in a oneness of "essence" (that which "makes up" the being known as God). Rather, it is found in oneness of love and purpose.[1] For faithful Mormons there is not only one god. There are several, in fact, many gods. "Many men say there is one God; the Father, the Son, and the Holy Ghost are only one God! I say that is a strange God anyhow. . . . All are to be crammed into one God."[2]

Brigham Henry Roberts was one of the presidents of the Council of Seventy and compiled a six-volume history of the Mormons. In one of his doctrinal essays, he summarizes the distinct Mormon teaching about God:

> The oneness of the Godhead, as described in the scriptures, never was intended to apply to the essence, but only to the perfections and other attributes. . . . The teaching of The Church offends against alleged orthodox doctrine in that when it affirms that absolute distinctness of the personages of the Godhead, it affirms that there is a plurality of Gods—three. . . . We affirm that there are three distinct personages in that Godhead and that their oneness consists only in a unity of mind, purpose, knowledge, wisdom, goodness, glory, etc.[3]

GOD WAS ONCE A MAN

The Mormon teaching about the nature or essence of God leads to the conclusion that God was once a human who has been exalted to the status of a god. Joseph Smith clearly taught this, and many other Mormon writers have expressed the same idea.

21

I am going to tell you how God came to be God. We have imagined and supposed that God was God from all eternity. I will refute that idea, and take away the veil, so that you may see. . . . It is the first principle of the Gospel to know for a certainty the character of God, and to know that we may converse with him as one man converses with another and that he was once a man like us; yea, that God himself, the Father of us all, dwelt on an earth, the same as Jesus Christ himself did; and I will show it from the Bible.[4]

More recently, a late president of the church, Joseph Fielding Smith, referred in his writings to a statement from a sermon of Joseph Smith that troubled some people: "Our Father in heaven at one time passed through a life and death and is an exalted man."[5]

ETERNAL PROGRESSION

If God could progress from human to divine being, it is then possible for all humans to achieve divinity if the right path is followed. To become a god, then, is the ultimate goal of every Mormon male. A woman also may achieve "godhood" but in a secondary role. She is never prayed to or called by name. Her role seems to be to produce billions of spirits for her husband's world.

Joseph Smith clearly taught that humans could ascend to divine being. "Here then, is eternal life—to know the only wise and true God; and you have got to learn how to be gods yourselves, and to be kings and priests to God, the same as all gods have done before you, namely by going from one small degree to another, and from a small capacity to a great one."[6] Or, as another early member of the LDS and former president wrote, "Remember that God our heavenly Father was perhaps a child, and mortal like we are, and rose step by step in the scale of progress, in the school of advancement; has moved forward and overcome until He has arrived at the point where He is now."[7]

This Mormon teaching of going from humanity to divinity is known as the doctrine of eternal progression. It is summed up in a frequently quoted phrase by the fifth president of the Mormon Church, Lorenzo Snow: "As man is, God once was; as God is, man may become."[8]

> "Remember that God our heavenly Father was perhaps a child, and mortal like we are, and rose step by step in the scale of progress, in the school of advancement; has moved forward and overcome until He has arrived at the point where He is now."
>
> —Orson Hyde, former LDS president

23

POLYTHEISM IN MORMONISM

We find then that Mormon teaching declares the existence of many gods. In addition to Father, Son, and Holy Spirit, there is an infinite number of other gods. Mormon writers such as Bruce R. McConkie make this Mormon teaching quite clear. "To us, speaking in the proper infinite sense, these three are the only Gods we worship. But in addition there is an infinite number of holy personages, drawn from worlds without number, who have passed on to exaltation and are thus gods."[9]

These gods, furthermore, have their own wives. An early apostle of the church, Orson Pratt, stated that each of the gods "has his own wife, or wives, which were given to him previous to his redemption, while yet in his mortal state."[10]

Joseph Smith declared that the plurality of gods has been a teaching of the church from its beginning. "I will preach on the plurality of Gods. . . . I wish to declare I have always and in all congregations when I have preached on the subject of the Deity, it has been on the plurality of Gods."[11]

Despite this clear teaching of the LDS church that has existed almost since its beginning, the average church member most often thinks of God in terms of the Father of Jesus Christ. This is the "popular" God of Mormonism. Some Mormons even seem to be unaware of the official teaching of the plurality of gods.

THE GOD OF THE BIBLE

Christian belief about the triune God is drawn only from the Bible. There is only one God (Deuteronomy 6:4; 1 Corinthians 8:4–6). Yet this God is three persons in one being. Each person is completely God, coequal and coeternal, sharing equally in the essence of Godhood (cf. Colossians 1:19). Each person shares in the creating, redeeming, and sanctifying work of the one God (Genesis 1:1; John 1:3; 16:12–15). Yet each person is distinct. The nature of God is a mystery, one that cannot be fully comprehended by human reason. This mystery serves to enhance the greatness of our God. Yet this teaching of the Trinity is essential to the Christian faith. As Jesus says, "And this is eternal life, that they know You the only true God, and Jesus Christ whom You have sent" (John 17:3).

God is revealed to us through Jesus Christ, God's Son. Christ came to earth to free humanity from sin (John 3:16; 1 John 4:9). The Spirit of God is the bearer of truth to all who believe (John 15:26; 1 Corinthians 12:3). All need to heed the warning of the apostle Paul that to exchange the glory of God for images of humans or other creatures is to become futile and foolish (Romans 1:21–23).

3 THE PLAN OF SALVATION

Many of the writings and statements of Mormon leaders sound like those of evangelical Christians. For example, in *What Mormons Think of Christ*, a very popular tract published by the Latter-day Saints, Elder Bruce McConkie writes, "Christ is our Redeemer and our Savior. Except for him there would be no salvation and no redemption, and unless men come unto him and accept him as their Savior, they cannot have eternal life in his presence."[1] This statement seems to be a correct expression of the Christian doctrine of salvation.

However, a closer look at Mormon teachings reveals different meanings for traditional Christian terms. When we look at the larger context, we discover the following statement in the same tract. "*Grace* is simply the mercy, the love and the condescension God has for his children, as a result of which he has ordained the plan of salvation *so that they may have power to progress and become like him.*"[2] The unique Mormon plan of salvation needs to be measured against the teachings of the Holy Bible.

A Mormon Hymn

by Eliza R. Snow

I had learned to call thee Father
By thy spirit from on high;
But, until the key of knowledge
Was restored, I knew not why;
In the heavens are parents
    single?
No, the thought makes reason
    stare.
Truth is reason; truth eternal
Tells me, I've a mother there.
— *Hymns,* The Church of Jesus
Christ of Latter-day Saints, no.
139.

PREMORTAL EXISTENCE

In Mormon belief, all people exist first as spirits in the spirit world.

In this premortal existence, the spirit children of the heavenly Father and Mother wait to be born into human bodies. It is necessary to go through an *earthly probation* to reach the celestial kingdom. In human bodies God's spirit children have the opportunity to follow the Mormon path of obedience to the law of eternal progression and prove they are worthy of entering the celestial kingdom. The celestial kingdom is the highest of the three "heavens" in Mormon teaching. Only those who are faithful to the teachings of Joseph Smith go into this kingdom. Eternal progression continues here as Mormons make their way to godhood.

To provide bodies for these bodiless spirits is an important good work for Mormons. Therefore, Mormon leaders oppose birth control and abortion. Also, the former practice of polygamy had been rationalized with this teaching of the need to give bodiless spirits a body-home.[3]

ON THE WAY TO THE CELESTIAL KINGDOM

Mormons speak a great deal about "free agency." Every person in his or her earthly probation decides whether to accept or reject the gospel according to Mormonism. To accept this gospel includes keeping various commands (ordinances). The basic ordinances are these:

a. faith—the action of believing in God;

b. repentance—feeling sorry for what evil one has done and ceasing it;

c. baptism—a contract with God in which one promises to keep the commandments of God;

d. accepting the gift of the Holy Spirit;

e. keeping commandments such as morality, loyalty, tithing, Word of Wisdom, duty, celestial marriage, etc.

Step-by-step the kingdom is reached by keeping commandments. The training manual for Mormon missionaries, *Uniform System for Teaching Families*, makes clear the emphasis the Latter-day Saints place on obedience and commandment keeping.

> No one can ever be saved in his [the heavenly Father's] kingdom without showing his faith by *obeying* the Lord's commandments.. . . If we fail to *keep* the Lord's commandments, we will not be permitted to live with him. Christ taught that we will go to different places after the resurrection, depending on how well we have *kept* his commandments.[4]

Faith is a command to be kept. To be baptized is a command to be kept. So also is receiving the Holy Spirit. "Individual sin must be eliminated by obedience to God's commandments."[5] A person works and lives so as to gain access to the celestial kingdom. In contrast to the Christian faith, the atonement of Jesus Christ does not answer for one's individual, personal sins, which are forgiven on the condition of repentance, baptism, and a good life by each individual Mormon.

THE CELESTIAL KINGDOM

30 Accept the gospel (as taught within Mormonism), keep the ordinances, and the celestial heaven is gained. The

celestial, the terrestrial, and the telestial are the three kingdoms in the afterlife. The terrestrial kingdom is for good
folks who live commendable lives, even if they do not
accept Mormon teachings. It is also for those somewhat
nominal Mormons (every church has nominal members)
who are "not valiant, but who are instead lukewarm in
their devotion to the Church and to righteousness."[6] The
telestial heaven is at the bottom—for those who live evil
lives and reject the gospel according to Joseph Smith. It
is even for those who are "sorcerers and adulterers, blas-
phemers and murderers."[7] Eternal progression goes on
within each of these kingdoms, but it is not possible to
move from one kingdom to another (either up or down).

Since even "terrible sinners" will spend eternity in at
least the lowest level of heaven, it is apparent that
Mormonism reserves the idea of a place of eternal dam-
nation for "those sons of perdition who deny the Son after
the Father has revealed him" (*Doctrine and Covenants*
76:43–44). Popularly it is sometimes believed that there
is such a place occupied only by the worst individuals.
Some believe that it is a place of torment where very evil
people suffer until they are purified enough to enter the
telestial kingdom.[8]

It was mentioned earlier in this chapter that Mormon theology often gives different meanings to traditional Christian terms. As another example, note how the Christian teaching of eternal or everlasting punishment is explained or taught in the Mormon church:

> We hear the question: "Do not the scriptures say that it is 'eternal punishment' and 'everlasting punishment'?" Yes, but let us not put a private interpretation on these terms. Let us correctly understand their meaning.
>
> Eternal punishment is God's punishment; everlasting punishment is God's punishment. In other words, it is the name of the punishment God inflicts, he being eternal in his nature.
>
> Whosoever, therefore, receives God's punishment receives eternal punishment, whether it is endured one hour, one day, one week, one year, or an age.[9]

One's eternal destiny is not gained immediately upon death. Rather, the souls of all people go into "the spirit world," an intermediary place. Here they remain until the resurrection from the dead. The "righteous spirits" inhabit a portion of the spirit world called "Paradise," from which they have access to the "Spirit Prison," the dwelling place of the spirits of the wicked (Alma 40:11–14, The Book of Mormon). There the wicked will have a chance to hear and accept the Their prison doors may be opened, and they set free by the ordinance of the baptism for the dead. Those that are in the flesh do vicarious work for their dead and become "saviors upon Mount Zion." (Morgan, *Plan of Salvation*, 23)

Mormon gospel because the "righteous spirits in paradise have been commissioned to carry the message of salvation to the wicked spirits in hell."[10] The "righteous spirits" are assisted by those still living on earth who go through a baptism for the dead (see Chapter 6).

THE ROLE OF JESUS CHRIST

Even though the Mormons claim to be the Church of Jesus Christ, in reality Jesus Christ plays a minor role in the Mormon plan of salvation. The Mormon tract *What Mormons Think of Christ* clearly shows Jesus' minor role in Mormon belief:

Adam brought temporal and spiritual death into the world. The atonement of Christ ransoms us from the effects of both temporal and spiritual

33

death. . . . The atonement of Christ ransoms all men from the effects of this temporal death in that all are resurrected, all are brought forth in immortality, and the bodies and the spirits of all men are united again inseparably . . . The atonement of Christ ransoms men from the effects of spiritual death in that by obedience to the laws and ordinances of the gospel they can be born again and have spiritual life. They can . . . live again in the presence of God, which life is called eternal life.[11]

In other words, Christ's atoning work results in two ways:

1. All people will rise from the dead—the effect of temporal death is overcome;
2. Christ's work makes it possible for a person to obey God's laws and go into the celestial kingdom (see previous section).

Notice that McConkie does not connect the forgiveness of sins and Christ's atoning work.

As mentioned in the quote at the beginning of this chapter, Mormons teach that the grace of God is "the mercy, the love and the condescension God has for his children" that led him to ordain the plan of salvation "so that they may have power to progress and become like him." "To be saved by grace alone," then, means that "all men

. . . without any act on their part. . . are resurrected and become immortal because of the atoning sacrifice of Christ."[12]

The biblical doctrine of justification by faith alone has been strongly denied by many Mormon leaders. Dr. James E. Talmage called it the sectarian dogma of justification by faith alone that has exercised an influence for evil since the early days of Christianity.[13] In the fifth edition of *Articles of Faith*, he calls justification by faith alone a most pernicious doctrine (p. 111).

OLD STORY—NEW SYMBOLS

Two Mormon leaders summarize the Mormon plan of salvation: "The gospel of Jesus Christ is called the plan of salvation. It is a system of rules by complying with which salvation may be obtained."[14] "By obedience to the principles of the gospel of Jesus Christ, he [man] prepares himself for the glorious exaltation held in reserve for those who worship God in spirit and truth."[15]

The Mormon plan of salvation is clearly based on doing certain good works. Follow certain laws, keep certain ordinances, and salvation is yours. The works may differ from those commanded to Israel in Old Testament times. They may differ from the activities required of the Muslim, the Buddhist, or the Hindu. But it is basically the same idea, couched in new symbols—human beings work, earn, and thus climb their way into the heavenly kingdom.

THE BIBLICAL PLAN OF SALVATION

Holy Scriptures teach the completeness of salvation in Jesus Christ. This salvation is a free gift of God apart from any human work or effort to obey certain rules or commands. "He saved us, not because of works done by us in righteousness, but according to His own mercy" (Titus 3:5). The grace of God brings people to faith as they hear the Good News of what God has done through Jesus Christ. Paul writes, "For by grace you have been saved through faith. And this is not your own doing; it is the gift of God, not a result of works, so that no one may boast" (Ephesians 2:8–9). God's grace is a mystery. Why is God so loving and gracious? Despite who we are or what we have done or failed to do, God offers perfect and completed salvation as a gift.

It is grace that lifts people to the new life in Christ. By God's grace we are empowered to live to God's glory (Ephesians 2:10). God's grace picks us up though we fail again and again. The apostle Paul makes it clear that this is not something we accomplish on our own: "Then what becomes of our boasting? It is excluded. By what kind of law? By a law of works? No, but by the law of faith. For we hold that one is justified by faith apart from works of the law" (Romans 3:27–28).

4 THE CHURCH— LOST AND RESTORED

CHRIST ESTABLISHED HIS CHURCH

According to Mormon teaching, Jesus established a well-organized church during His earthly ministry. It was structured like the Mormon Church today. The twelve apostles were the foundation. As the LDS grew, bishops and elders were ordained, and offices in the priesthood were filled. The Aaronic and Melchizedek priesthoods formed the source of church authority.

The priesthood was first given to Adam and passed from father to son. It is the directing agency between God and humans. In the priesthood one receives guidance for oneself and for the group, and carries the authority to speak for God. Only those who share in the power of the priesthood can teach with authority. With the priesthood comes the authority to administer the ordinances of life and salvation, acts that are valid not only on earth but also in heaven. These include acts such as marriages, temple work (including baptism for the dead), the endowments, sealing, etc. The Mormon Church cannot exist without the priesthood. Since Mormons believe that only the Mormon Church has the priesthood, by implication they believe also that the acts, rites, and ceremonies performed by priests and ministers outside the Mormon Church are invalid—a point explicitly made about baptism.

However, it is interesting that David Whitmer, one of three witnesses to the Book of Mormon, said, "This matter of 'priesthood' . . . originated in the mind of Sidney Rigdon . . . [and] was introduced into the LDS almost two years after its beginning—and after we had baptized and confirmed about two thousand souls into the church."[1]

The book *Mormonism—Shadow or Reality* is an excellent resource of primary documentation from Mormon publications and authors. In this work, the Tanners clearly show that neither the Aaronic nor the Melchizedek priesthoods were included in the original revelations Joseph Smith claimed to receive, which were recorded in the *Book of Commandments*, the forerunner of *Doctrine and Covenants.*

Women are not permitted to hold the priesthood. "Women may enjoy every blessing and benefit of the priesthood through a properly ordained priesthood holder [their husbands]."[2] Motherhood is considered a gift equal in importance and power to the priesthood.

It wasn't until 1978 that men of nonwhite races were allowed to receive the priesthood. In that year, Spencer Kimball, the twelfth president/prophet of the Mormon Church, received the revelation that "every faithful, worthy man in the Church may receive the holy priesthood . . . without regard for race or color."[3]

The Aaronic priesthood handles the secular affairs of the church. These priests also have special responsibility for the poor, the widows, and the orphans. There are four offices in this priesthood: deacons (ages 12–14); teachers (ages 16–17); priests (ages 17–18); and bishop.

The Melchizedek priesthood has responsibility for the spiritual ordinances of the church. The duties of the lesser Aaronic priesthood are also included in it. In the Melchizedek priesthood there are six offices: elder (age 19 upward); seventy (spreading the gospel); high priest (source for all higher church officials); patriarch (giver of blessings); apostles (twelve men who regulate the affairs of the church); and presiding high priest (source for the Quorum of the Presidency of the Church).

THE CHURCH AND PRIESTHOOD LOST

The Mormon Church teaches that for a few years after Christ's ascension, the church remained fully organized and intact. But then a universal apostasy (falling away from the truth) took place. Gradually the church lost its true marks. The Scriptures were altered, and when the apostles were killed, they were not replaced. "At last, about six hundred years after Christ, the Gospel laws and ordinances had become so completely warped that it was as if the church had departed from the earth."[4] Here, then, is the reason for the existence of the Mormon Church: God reestablishing His true church on earth. All other churches are in a state of apostasy.

> With the loss of the apostles and other righteous priesthood holders, the authority of God to run his church and perform his ordinances was lost from the earth. . . . Except for The Church of Jesus Christ of Latter-day Saints, contemporary Christian churches do not have God's authority to act in his name.[5]

"What does the Christian world know about God? Nothing. . . . Why, so far as the things of God are concerned, they are the veriest fools; they know neither God nor the things of God." (John Taylor, "How to Know the Things of God," in *Journal of Discourses*, ed. G. W. Evans and John Grimshaw [Liverpool: Horace S. Eldredge, 1871], 13:225.)

It was up to God to restore the church so that people might come into the fold once again. The way for restoration was prepared by such people as Luther, Calvin, Knox, and other reformers. The Renaissance, modern inventions, and the Constitution of the United States also played a role in preparing for the restoration of the church.

THE CHURCH RESTORED

Mormons also claim that the Church, as it was established by Jesus Christ, was restored to this earth through Joseph Smith Jr. It has the same basic structure, offices, and basis for authority. It is a visible institution, with an organizational chart that matches the organizational chart supposedly developed by Jesus. It includes apostles and high priests, seventies and prophets, evangelists and patriarchs, pastors or bishops, elders and teachers, priests and deacons.

As a result of the Lord's working through Joseph Smith, the church of Jesus Christ was once again established on the earth. It is directed today by a prophet and apostles just as the church was when the Savior was on earth. . . . These apostles and the prophet are the Savior's messengers here on earth, and following their teachings is very important.[6]

Manuals used by Mormon missionaries usually place considerable emphasis on the organization of the Church. They strive to convince potential members that the Church of Latter-day Saints is the same as that established by Jesus Christ.

THE CHURCH AND CHRIST'S PROMISE

Many questions could be raised concerning the Mormon teachings about the Church, but three particularly stand out. Is the true Church of Christ an institution with an organizational chart and a corporate structure? Did the Lord Jesus truly organize His Church in the way the LDS is organized today? Was the Church really lost for over one thousand years and in need of restoration by Joseph Smith Jr.?

The Church in its essential nature is not an institution; it is people called to faith in Jesus Christ. "Where two or three are gathered in My name, there am I among them" (Matthew 18:20). The Church is to be found in factories and on farms, in offices and in classrooms, in homes and in apartments. Wherever the people of Christ are laboring and loving, serving and celebrating, witnessing and praying, there is the Church. Christ nourishes His people through Word and Sacrament, for He is the vine and they are the branches. This is the New Testament picture of the Church.

Over the centuries Christ's people have organized themselves in various ways for the strengthening of their faith and the spreading of the Gospel. There have been legalistic theocracies and democratic organizations. Some were good; some led to abuses and corruption. But the people of God remained; the Church did not disappear.

There is little evidence that the New Testament Church had any highly developed organizational structure. The Book of Acts mentions minimal structure in the Early Church. We read that assistants were chosen "to serve tables" so that the apostles could attend to "preaching the word of God" (Acts 6). The apostles were called to go into the world to preach the Gospel, not to form an organization. In the period of the New Testament that followed, the structure continued to change. However, the one office that the New Testament does establish in the church is the Office of the Holy Ministry. Yet this office is missing from the LDS structure.[7]

> For as the rain and the snow come down from heaven and do not return there but water the earth, making it bring forth and sprout, giving seed to the sower and bread to the eater, so shall My word be that goes out from My mouth; it shall not return to Me empty, but it shall accomplish that which I purpose, and shall succeed in the thing for which I sent it. (Isaiah 55:10–11)

Did the Church really disappear from the earth for over one thousand years? Institutions may have been corrupt and failed in their mission, but the people of God were still there. Sometimes the people of God were highly visible; sometimes they were underground. (Elijah once thought he was the only follower of God left on earth.) Down through the centuries people continued to hear and believe the Word. That is why men like Girolamo Savonarola, Jan Hus, Martin Luther, and John Calvin could rise to reform the Church of their day. God's promises are true. As long as the earth remains, the Church remains also.

45

5 THE GOLDEN PLATES AND THE GOLDEN CASKET

In his hymn "O Word of God Incarnate," William W. How refers to the Holy Bible as "the golden casket where gems of truth are stored." Mormons claim the Book of Mormon originated in some mysterious golden plates (see chapter 1). Are gems of truth stored here too? Or is it just a religious book fabricated by human beings?

The Book of Mormon was a mutation in the evolution of American literature, a curious sport, at once sterile and potent. Although it bred no imitators outside Mormonism and was ignored by literary critics, it brought several hundred thousand immigrants to America in the 19th century. The 20th century sees the distribution of thousands of copies each year. For more than a hundred years missionaries have heralded it throughout the world as religious history second only to the Bible.[1]

TRANSLATING THE GOLDEN PLATES

Emma Smith, Joseph's wife, was the first to assist Joseph as a scribe as he translated the golden plates. Her scribal activity was in accord with the revelation Joseph had received. "And thou shalt go with him at the time of his going, and be unto him for a scribe" (*Doctrines and Covenants* 25:6). To translate the first 116 pages, Joseph used stones that he claimed came with the plates. He called them Urim and Thummim. For the rest of the translation he used his "little dark seer stone." Emma said Joseph would translate from the plates without even removing the small linen tablecloth that covered them. Joseph would stare into his "stones" and begin dictating. She would write as he spoke.

In April 1828, Martin Harris began to assist with the writing of Joseph's translation. The Smiths were now living in Harmony, New York. A rope divided the room and a blanket was flung across it. Joseph sat on one side, staring into his stones. Harris sat on the other side at a table. Martin was warned not to look at the plates or even at Joseph. If he did, the wrath of God would strike him down.

Progress was slow, and after two months only 116 pages were completed—including the pages dictated to Emma. The book fascinated Harris, but his wife was an outspoken skeptic of the venture. Martin begged Joseph to permit him to show these pages to his wife. Joseph reluctantly gave his permission. Martin took the pages home to show them to his wife, and she promptly stole them. She challenged Joseph to translate them over again. Knowing that to retranslate would invite comparison between the two translations, Joseph refused to fall into the trap.

To solve the dilemma, Joseph claimed the Lord provided a set of small plates (the book of Nephi), which covered the exact period of history as the stolen 116 pages. The record was kept complete without running the risk of retranslating the missing section.

In April 1829, Oliver Cowdery, a young schoolmaster, took over the task of writing down the translation. The pace now quickened. The translation was finished in July 1829 and published in early 1830.

Joseph claimed that the language of the golden plates was an altered, or "reformed," Egyptian. However, Egyptian hieroglyphics remained untranslatable until 1837 when the grammar worked out from the Rosetta stone was made public. Martin Harris attempted to have

Joseph's claim verified by Charles Anthon, a linguist at Columbia College, New York. Anthon, however, vigorously denied lending any credence to the genuineness of the characters. Smith later would describe the Book of Mormon as "the most correct of any book on Earth and the keystone of our religion." Detractors through the years have dismissed Smith's story as religious fantasy and the book itself as a clumsy reworking of the King James Version of the Bible.[7]

Confusion exists regarding how Joseph received the translation. Martin Harris once claimed that Joseph saw the English translation under the foreign characters. Mormons today claim Smith was given only the essence of the translation, not a word-for-word translation. This is important to maintain the supposed authenticity of the Book of Mormon, since at least three thousand changes have been made between the original translation and the text that is used today.

WHAT'S IT ALL ABOUT?

The Book of Mormon claims to be a history of early America. It describes three different migrations of people from the Holy Land to America. Jared and his family left the Holy Land around the time of the tower of Babel. By 600 BC they had killed each other off in fratricidal warfare. Around 585 BC the Mulekites left Jerusalem and settled in a land called Zarahemla. They obtained a record of the Jaredites from Coriantumr, the only survivor of the Jaredites. About the same time, a Jew, Lehi, took his family from Jerusalem and landed on one of the American continents. Two of his six sons, Laman and Lemuel, were evil-tempered and sinful. God cursed them and their descendants with a dark skin. The other four sons—Nephi, Sam, Jacob, and Joseph—begat white children.

Eventually the Nephites discovered the Mulekites and joined with them, the combined race being known as the Nephites. The descendants of Laman and Lemuel were known as the Lamanites. For centuries the two races fought, but about the time of Christ there was a golden age of peace. The living Christ visited these people and at that time established His church in the Western world.

But the peace was short lived. Between AD 200 and 300, war between the races resumed. After each battle, the dead were "heaped up upon the face of the earth, and they were covered with a shallow covering." This was Joseph Smith's explanation of the Indian mounds found in parts of the United States (which had caused much curiosity in Joseph's day). According to Smith, the largest mounds mark the site of the last great battle some time after AD 400. The Lamanites (dark-skinned race) destroyed the Nephites (white-skinned race). Thus only the Lamanites greeted Columbus when he arrived in 1492.

Fortunately, the prophet Mormon had kept the history of the nation on golden plates and had given the plates to his son, Moroni, the only Nephite to survive. Prior to his death Moroni buried these plates on Hill Cumorah, where Joseph was led to find them fourteen centuries later. This is the story of the Book of Mormon.

PECULIARITIES

To the average reader the content of the Book of Mormon would seem rather strange. The reader would discover references to various items only available to nineteenth-century Europeans and Americans. For example, the Nephites had a brass ball with two spindles to direct the sailing of their ships—in reality, a nineteenth-century com-pass. The Nephites also produced wheat and barley (crops common at the time of Joseph Smith), rather than the maize and potatoes of Native Americans. Mormon critics contend that it is virtually impossible that records written fourteen hundred years *prior* to the time of Joseph

Smith should detail specific social, political, and religious concerns unique to nineteenth-century America.[3]

The Book of Mormon and the King James Version of the Bible have many parallels. In fact, more than a hundred names found in the book are biblical names, sometimes with a slight change in spelling. About twenty-five thousand words in the Book of Mormon are copied from the King James Old Testament, with another two thousand from the New Testament. Some slight changes have been made in the wording to forestall any criticism about how an ancient American prophet could use the exact text of the King James Bible. In their thorough study of this topic, *The Case against Mormonism* (Salt Lake City: Utah Lighthouse Ministry, 1968), Jerald and Sandra Tanner have listed more than four hundred verses and portions of verses from the New Testament quoted in the Book of Mormon.

Archaeological evidence—rather, the lack of it—also presents a problem for the Book of Mormon. Much evidence supports what is recorded in the Bible. Although Mormon missionaries continue to claim that archaeological evidence exists to support the "history" recorded in the Book of Mormon, none has ever been found. Both the Smithsonian Institute and the National Geographic Society have denied Mormon missionary claims.

In other words, no Book of Mormon cities have ever been located, no Book of Mormon person, place, nation, or name has been found, no Book of Mormon artifacts, no Book of Mormon scriptures, no Book of Mormon inscriptions, no Book of Mormon gold plates—nothing which demonstrates the Book of Mormon is anything other than myth or invention has ever been found.[4]

WITNESSES

The followers of Joseph Smith begged to see the golden plates, but Joseph told them they had been taken into heaven once the translation was finished. However, Oliver Cowdery, David Whitmer, and Martin Harris were finally given a vision of the plates. All three told different versions of their experience, and all three also eventually quarreled with Joseph and left his church. Cowdery and Harris were later rebaptized and readmitted into the church.

When questioned about the plates by a Palmyra lawyer, Martin Harris said, "I did not see them as I do that pencil-case, yet I saw them with the eye of faith; I saw them just as distinctly as I see anything around me—though at the time they were covered with a cloth." Harris is the same witness who is identified in two revelations given to Joseph (*Doctrines and Covenants* 3:12–13; 10:1, 6–7) as a *wicked man* for his part in the first 116 pages of the translation.[5]

Eight other witnesses also claimed they were shown the plates. Most printings of the Book of Mormon include the separate statements of the three and the eight witnesses.

THE SOURCE

Skeptics of the divine origin of the Book of Mormon have proposed various theories about its origination. Among the most popular is the theory that it is the plagiarism of an old manuscript written by Solomon Spalding, a congregationalist preacher who died in 1816. But the only Spalding manuscript that has ever been found is a florid, sentimental, Indian romance.[6] Other critics insist that the Book of Mormon is the result of a demented mind; these critics insist that Joseph suffered from delusions.

The most realistic approach would be to credit Joseph Smith as the author. He had a fertile imagination and a fair amount of learning. Joseph had a keen interest in what was being said and written about religion in his day. The Tanners identify the close relationship between the work and teaching of Alexander Campbell (to whom both the Disciples of Christ and the LDS trace their beginnings) and that of Joseph Smith.[7]

In addition to the Book of Mormon, Latter-day Saints have three other basic sources for their teachings: *Doctrine and Covenants, The Pearl of Great Price,* and the King James Version of the Bible, "insofar as it is translated correctly."

In *No Man Knows My History*, Fawn Brodie makes a good case for many current issues of the times being included in the book, some of them taking place as the book was being "written." She writes,

> Any theory of the origin of *The Book of Mormon* that spotlights the prophet and blacks out the stage on which he performed is certain to be a distortion. For the book can best be explained, not by Joseph's ignorance nor by his delusions, but by his responsiveness to the provincial opinions of his time. He had neither the diligence nor the constancy to master reality, but his mind was open to all intellectual influences, from whatever province they might blow.[8]

55

ADDITIONAL AUTHORITIES

Doctrine and Covenants is probably the most important of the three. It contains revelations given to Joseph Smith and some of his successors in the presidency of the church. Here one will find most of the doctrines accepted by the Mormons. There are directions and beliefs concerning baptism and the sacrament (section 20); concerning the three heavens (section 76); and the much-quoted Word of Wisdom (section 89).

However, some teachings of *Doctrine and Covenants* do not agree with present-day teachings and practices of the Mormon Church—for example, God is the same and does not change (section 76), salvation is through faith, and God is one (section 20). In addition, *Doctrine and Covenants* and the Book of Mormon sometimes disagree.

The Pearl of Great Price, a third source of Mormon teaching, is purported to be the *Book of Abraham* found among some Egyptian manuscripts and also translated by Joseph Smith. It contains teachings on the plurality of gods, populated stars, and the creation of the earth out of existing materials. Various scholars have confirmed that the papyri from which *The Pearl of Great Price* was supposedly translated is nothing more than an Egyptian burial text.

Joseph Smith attempted his own translation of the Bible and called it the *Inspired Version of the Bible*. By most scholarly standards it is regarded as a very poor translation. The King James Version of the Bible, "insofar as it is translated correctly," is most often used by Mormons today. Frequently, however, KJV Bibles produced for Mormons include extensive excerpts from Joseph Smith's translation.

The Mormons also accept the idea of continuing revelation. New revelations can be given to the church at any time—for example, the revelation putting an end to the practice of polygamy and the revelation opening the priesthood to black males. However, the serious Bible student will put all "additional revelation" to the test suggested by the apostle Paul in Galatians 1:8: "But even if we or an angel from heaven should preach to you a gospel contrary to the one we preached to you, let him be accursed."

6 UNUSUAL PRACTICES AND BELIEFS

It is easy to be fascinated by those aspects of Mormonism that are different from mainline Christian beliefs and practices. But to be as complete as possible some of the more unusual aspects of Mormonism should be touched upon.

LEADERSHIP IN THE CHURCH

The Mormon Church is unique among larger American churches in that it does not have a professional clergy trained in theology. At the local level, a "bishop" takes the leadership role. The bishop is chosen from the membership of the ward (similar to a parish or congregation). He has to come through the ranks from deacon to the present position. He continues to support himself and his family through his chosen vocation. The bishop of the local ward is assisted by several counselors and a large number of other voluntary workers.

A number of wards comprise a "stake." Stakes are presided over by a stake president. A very structured hierarchy continues beyond this level of authority all the way up to the president of the church. None of the Mormon leaders are specifically trained as theologians. Success in the business or professional world seems to be one of the major requisites for higher church leadership. Only at the higher levels of church leadership can individuals receive their livelihood through the church.

POLYGAMY

One thing most people know about the LDS is that at one time the practice of men having more than one wife was encouraged. There is evidence that polygamy was practiced already during the Nauvoo days of the church. Fawn Brodie lists the names of forty-eight women considered to be plural wives of Joseph Smith. Many of these women were only "sealed" to Joseph for eternity. They did not live with Joseph in his lifetime.

After the Mormons were safely in Utah, Brigham Young publicly revealed the doctrine of plural marriage or polygamy. It commanded those who could support more than one wife to take more. Acceptance of new wives was required on the part of the first wife.

The practice of plural marriage brought much persecution to Mormons in Utah. Finally, in October 1890, in order to gain statehood for Utah, President Wilford Woodruff forbade Mormons to practice polygamy. Interestingly, Woodruff's statement does not actually condemn the doctrine of plural marriage. It rather advises them to "refrain from contracting any marriage forbidden by the law of the land."

The Church of Jesus Christ of Latter-day Saints does not practice or condone plural marriage today. However, various "orthodox" Mormon sects do continue to follow this practice, claiming that God should be obeyed rather than men.

TEMPLE RITE AND GARMENTS

Mormon temples are found throughout the United States, Canada, and in many parts of the world. Only active members of the church may enter the temples. A number of secret rituals take place in the temples, including baptism for the dead, marriage for eternity, and the receiving of endowments (special blessings).

Some non-Mormon critics see a strong connection between Mormon temple rituals and Masonic temple rituals. They note the "coincidence" that shortly after joining the Masonic Lodge, Joseph Smith received revelations about rituals to be used in the Mormon Church, especially the endowment ceremony. It would seem that Smith developed his religion as he went along. Of course, Mormon leaders such as Roberts (*A Scrap Book*, 2:423–24) and authors such as McConkie (*Mormon Doctrine*, 334) offer a different explanation for the source of the temple rituals and ceremonies, namely, the *Book of Abraham*.

There also seems to be a connection between Mormonism and Masonry in terms of special clothing worn by those who go through the temple rituals. Mormon garments include a small apron (containing secret symbols) similar to the apron/lambskin worn by Masons.

Active Mormons are usually buried in their temple garments. Those members of the church who have gone through some of the temple rituals are also privileged to wear a special kind of undergarment as part of their daily dress. These undergarments

"We feel that at least part of the temple ceremWny came from Freemasonry. In fact, the similarities between the temple ceremony and the ritual of the Masons are rather startling." (Jerald and Sandra Tanner, *Mormonism— Shadow or Reality* [Salt Lake City: Utah Lighthouse Ministry, 1972], 486)

have a number of symbols—one on each breast, one at the navel, and one at the right knee. They are worn by both men and women (with some modifications) and are considered very sacred by faithful Mormons. The symbols are reminders of the temple rituals and endowments.[1]

BAPTISM FOR THE DEAD

The Mormon Church encourages their living members to be baptized *for* those who have died outside the Mormon faith. This practice leads many Mormons to study their family tree and is the primary reason for the extensive genealogical records kept by the Mormon Church. This baptism may be by proxy or by the living relative. Baptism for the dead does not coerce the dead into accepting the religion of Joseph Smith. Rather it removes obstacles to make it easier for the deceased to accept Mormon teachings. This second chance is possible, because all who die enter the intermediary "spirit world" where they await the second coming of Christ.

MARRIAGE FOR ETERNITY

Marriages performed or "sealed" in the temple do not end upon one party's death. Such marriages endure for eternity. Children are also "sealed" to the couple for eternity. It is permissible for Mormon men to be sealed to more than one woman. A woman can have only one valid sealing to a man on the records.

WORD OF WISDOM

In some ways the Word of Wisdom, section 89 in *Doctrine and Covenants*, dominates daily life for the Mormon faithful. This section is the guide for the "clean living" for which Mormons are noted. It condemns the use of tobacco, alcohol, and other strong drinks, as well as hot drinks. It specifically advises against the regular use of meat, except "in times of winter, or of cold, or famine." However, few Mormons seem to take this part of the health code seriously. The saints who follow the Word of Wisdom are promised "health in the navel and marrow to their bones." The Word of Wisdom assures them that they will find "wisdom and great treasures of knowledge" and that they "shall run and not be weary, and shall walk and not faint" (*Doctrines and Covenants* 89:18–20).

BAPTISM AND THE SACRAMENT

Baptism is one of the ordinances that must be kept to attain salvation. "A person must be baptized if he is to be saved in the celestial kingdom."[2] Children are not baptized before the age of eight. Mormons baptize by immersion only in the name of the Father and of the Son and of the Holy Ghost (*Doctrines and Covenants* 20:73). The use of the names of the three persons of the triune God gives the appearance of a proper Christian Baptism. However, as has been shown, the Mormon Church does not confess the Trinity but rather a belief in three gods.

The Sacrament (Holy Communion) is offered in most wards each Sunday at a sacrament meeting. *Doctrine and Covenants* states that wine is to be used, but Mormons commonly use water instead. Sunday morning activities at a Mormon ward usually begin with priesthood meetings, followed by Sunday School, and then the sacrament meeting.

THE MORMON AND THE NONWHITE RACES

Since the Book of Mormon espouses the theory that Native Americans are part of the Jewish race, early Mormons looked with great favor upon them. Originally, Mormons made valiant attempts to convert Native Americans to Mormonism. To some extent these efforts have continued in modern times, especially among tribes in the Southwest, but with little success. Not too many Native Americans have been attracted to the teachings of Joseph Smith.

Black people were long considered a cursed race by Mormons. But a recent revelation (see chapter 4) has permitted black males to become priests. Again, not too many black people have been attracted to Mormonism. The Mormons have been most successful among Hawaiians, Pacific Islanders, and New Zealand Maoris. It was frequently reported in the past that Mormon missionaries promised people with brown-colored skin that if they joined the church, they would be white in the next life.

7 How to Talk to Your Mormon Neighbors about the One True God

Christians can learn much from their Mormon neighbors even while disagreeing with them on many points of religious belief. Many Mormons are very dedicated to their religion. They voluntarily give extensive amounts of their time to lead and participate in the many activities that are part of the average ward chapel. Keep in mind that nonprofessional volunteers lead most of the ward activities, including the sacrament meetings and the teaching of classes. Most active Mormons tithe from their income, and many give even beyond the tithe.

Mormons are widely known for their evangelistic zeal. Many Mormon young men and women interrupt their lives to spend two years doing missionary work for their church. Some older and retired couples volunteer their skills in some mission field. Mormons are also well trained to work in their home communities to spread the gospel according to Joseph Smith.

Mormons project an image of clean living and strong family values. Most wards have a strong youth program that appeals to young people in the community. Although most Mormons would be considered laity, there generally is a high degree of knowledge concerning basic church doctrine. The Mormon community tends to emphasize education, music, other arts, health and body care, and moral living.

As Christians, we should be prepared to speak to the Mormon missionaries who come to our door. "Always [be] prepared to make a defense to anyone who asks you for a reason for the hope that is in you; yet do it with gentleness and respect" (1 Peter 3:15).

"Rather, speaking the truth in love, we are to grow up in every way into Him who is the head, into Christ" (Ephesians 4:15).

How does a committed Christian respond to a Mormon neighbor or friend? What follows is admittedly subjective but is born out of the observations and experiences of the author.

SOME SUGGESTED DON'TS

When you are speaking with your Mormon neighbors, avoid the temptation to get involved in the discussion of peripheral matters. Such conversations might be interesting, but they often miss making a true Christian witness. Try rather to get to the heart of the Christian faith: Jesus Christ and the salvation He offers through grace.

Make every effort to avoid irrelevant religious arguments. Any argument focused on winning points is a losing activity. If you gain the most "points," you will only gain the ill will of the loser. If your opponent scores more "points," you will have lost the purpose of your discussion. The Lord does not ask us to win arguments, but to confess our faith in a loving and straightforward manner.

> The Lord does not ask us to win arguments, but to confess our faith in a loving and straightforward manner.

One often finds a wide variety of religious opinion among Mormons. While knowledgeable about the basics of the faith, many Mormons are not aware of the "deeper" teachings of Mormon theology. They do not have a professional clergy to direct and guide them. Depend on reliable resources for information. Be cautious of non-Mormons who have an axe to grind or who propose the use of "trap" questions. Such questions only cause anger and frustration and do not show love and concern for another human being.

SOME SUGGESTED DOS

The truth of God's love and grace in Jesus Christ should form the center of your witness to Mormons. God's grace is the free gift of His forgiveness, love, and new life through Jesus Christ. God's grace cannot be earned. God initiates the giving because He loves us. Humans tend to want to share in the glory of gaining salvation. As has been seen, Mormonism replaces the Gospel with a new law. The grace of God in Jesus Christ needs to be clearly proclaimed.

It is helpful to be familiar with the teachings of the LDS. Such knowledge will aid in understanding Mormon friends and neighbors and help you to witness to them. There is no better witness than one's own life. Be active in a Christian church and know clearly the fundamental teachings of the Christian faith. Learn to articulate them. Develop good Christian traditions in your home. Live the Church Year and celebrate the richness of each Church season. One does not need to be super pious. Enjoy life. Live it freely under the forgiving grace of God. Celebrate!

Your faith can be most meaningfully shared when mutual trust and concern are present. Don't hesitate to become friends with Mormon neighbors and relatives. Share your deepest feelings, hopes, and beliefs. A degree of intimacy and trust is the most fertile ground for witnessing.

Respect the rights and beliefs of others. Do not make pawns of others or use them as talking points to score debate points. Recognize others as human beings and not simply objects for conversation.

God can use you best when you share yourself at the deepest level. Let your love and concern for your Mormon neighbor show through. That's what God asks of you. "Beloved, let us love one another, for love is from God" (1 John 4:7). God bless your loving and witnessing to the honor and glory of His name.

THE ARTICLES OF FAITH OF THE CHURCH OF JESUS CHRIST OF LATTER-DAY SAINTS

1. We believe in God the eternal Father and in His Son Jesus Christ and in the Holy Ghost.

2. We believe that men will be punished for their own sins and not for Adam's transgression.

3. We believe that through the atonement of Christ all mankind may be saved by obedience to the laws and ordinances of the Gospel.

4. We believe that the first principles and ordinance of the Gospel are (1) faith in the Lord Jesus Christ; (2) repentance; (3) baptism by immersion for the remission of sins; (4) laying on of hands for the gift of the Holy Ghost.

5. We believe that a man must be called of God by prophecy and by the laying on of hands, by those who are in authority, to preach the Gospel and administer in the ordinances thereof.

6. We believe in the same organization that existed in the primitive church; viz., apostles, prophets, pastors, teachers, evangelists, etc.

7. We believe in the gift of tongues, prophecy, revelation, visions, healing, interpretation of tongues, etc.

8. We believe the Bible to be the word of God, as far as it is translated correctly; we also believe *The Book of Mormon* to be the word of God.

9. We believe all that God has revealed, all that He does now reveal, and we believe that He will yet reveal many great and important things pertaining to the kingdom of God.

10. We believe in the literal gathering of Israel and in the restoration of the Ten Tribes; that Zion will be built upon this [the American] continent; that Christ will reign personally upon the earth; and that the earth will be renewed and receive its paradisiacal glory.

11. We claim the privilege of worshiping Almighty God according to the dictates of our own conscience, and allow all men the same privilege, let them worship how, where, or what they may.

12. We believe in being subject to kings, presidents, rulers, and magistrates, in obeying, honoring, and sustaining the law.

13. We believe in being honest, true, chaste, benevolent, virtuous, and in doing good to all men; indeed we may say that we follow the admonition of Paul, "We believe all things, we hope all things, we have endured many things, and hope to be able to endure all things. If there is anything virtuous, lovely, or of good report, or praiseworthy, we seek after these things."[1]

APPENDIX B

BRANCHES OF MORMONISM

The Church of Jesus Christ of Latter-day Saints: The largest branch of Mormonism. Headquarters: Salt Lake City, Utah. Founded under the leadership of Brigham Young, who led his followers from Nauvoo, Illinois, to the Salt Lake Valley. This book is exclusively about this group.

Reorganized Church of Jesus Christ of Latter Day Saints: The bulk of Mormons who do not accept the leadership of the Salt Lake City organization. Headquarters: Independence, Missouri. The reorganized Mormon Church claims to be the true successor of the church founded by Joseph Smith. It denies the polytheism espoused by the Salt Lake City Mormons and denies that Joseph Smith ever taught or practiced polygamy. The founders of this group, among them Emma Smith, Joseph's brother (William), and Joseph's son (Young Joseph), refused to accept the leadership of Brigham Young. They remained in the Midwest where their strength remains.

The Church of Christ (Temple Lot): Founded in Bloomington, Illinois, by a small group who believed that the Temple Lot in Independence, Missouri, will be the center of the priesthood during the restoration. They own legal rights to three acres of ground and spend much energy in maintaining the legal rights. They repudiate the doctrine of baptism for the dead, polygamy, and the elevation of man to godhood.

The Church of Jesus Christ (Bickertonites): Founded by William Bickerton in Pittsburgh, Pennsylvania. This group and the following one rejected the leadership of Brigham Young and the teachings of polygamy, polytheism, and baptism for the dead.

The Church of Jesus Christ (Cutlerites): Founded by Alphaeus Cutler in 1853. He believed the temple was to be built at Nauvoo, Illinois.

The Church of Jesus Christ of Latter Day Saints (Strangites): J. J. Strang maintained that he was the true successor of Joseph Smith. He was a Wisconsin lawyer of ability and ambition. He was crowned "King in Zion" by his followers on Beaver Island in Lake Michigan and had national political ambitions. His group was polygamous and indulged in secret orders. In 1856, he was shot to death by two men. The group has nearly died out.

Others: Sidney Rigdon, Lyman Wight, Austin Cowles, James Emmet, Gladden Bishop, George M. Hinkle, W. E. M'Lellin, Martin Harris, and John C. Whitmer all, at various times, started groups on their own.

RESOURCES

The Book of Mormon. Salt Lake City: The Church of Jesus Christ of Latter-day Saints. Various editions have been published.

The Doctrine and Covenants of The Church of Jesus Christ of Latter-day Saints. Salt Lake City: The Church of Jesus Christ of Latter-day Saints, 1948. Various other editions have been published.

Ankerberg, John, and John Weldon. *Cult Watch.* Eugene, OR: Harvest House, 1991.

Brodie, Fawn M. *No Man Knows My History: The Life of Joseph Smith, the Mormon Prophet.* 2nd enlarged edition. New York: Alfred A. Knopf, 1995.

Cowdrey, Wayne L., Howard A. Davis, and Arthur Vanick. *Who Really Wrote the Book of Mormon? The Spalding Enigma.* St. Louis: Concordia, 2005.

Hinckley, Gordon B. *What of the Mormons? Including a Short History of the Church of Jesus Christ of Latter-day Saints.* Salt Lake City: The Church of Jesus Christ of Latter-day Saints, 1954.

O'Dea, Thomas F. *The Mormons.* Chicago: University of Chicago Press, 1958.

Smith, Joseph Fielding. *Doctrines of Salvation I, II, III.* Edited by Bruce R. McConkie. 3 volumes. Salt Lake City: Bookcraft, 1954.

Tanner, Jerald, and Sandra Tanner. *Mormonism—Shadow or Reality.* 5th ed. Salt Lake City: Utah Lighthouse Ministry, 1987.

Widtsoe, John A. *Priesthood and Church Government.* Salt Lake City: Deseret, 1965.

TRACTS AND OTHER PUBLICATIONS

McConkie, Bruce R. "What Mormons Think of Christ." Salt Lake City: The Church of Jesus Christ of Latter-day Saints, 1976.

The Commission on Theology and Church Relations. *The Church of Jesus Christ of the Latter-day Saints.* St. Louis: The Lutheran Church—Missouri Synod, 2008.

Plan of Salvation. Salt Lake City: The Church of Jesus Christ of Latter-day Saints, 1978.

Uniform System for Teaching Families. Salt Lake City: The Church of Jesus Christ of Latter-day Saints, 1981.

INTERNET RESOURCES

www.lds.org (See especially their "Gospel Library" section for more LDS tracts regarding their beliefs.)

www.mormon.org

www.lcms.org (The Commission on Theology and Church Relations [CTCR] has provided some excellent summaries and theological evaluations of many modern cults.)

NOTES

CHAPTER ONE

1. Jeffrey L. Sheler and Betsy Wagner, "Latter-Day Struggles," *U.S. News & World Report* (September 28, 1992): 73–74.

2. For an overview of the religious climate in the early 1800s, see Thomas F. O'Dea, *The Mormons* (University of Chicago, 1957).

3. *The Doctrine and Covenants of The Church of Jesus Christ of Latter-day Saints* (Salt Lake City: The Church of Jesus Christ of Latter-day Saints, 1948), 25.

4. O'Dea, *The Mormons*, 69.

CHAPTER TWO

1. Samuel O. Bennion, *Fundamental Principles of the Gospel* (Independence, MO: Zion's Printing and Publishing), 22.

2. Joseph Smith and Edwin F. Parry, *Joseph Smith's Teachings* (Salt Lake City: The Deseret, 1912), 55ff.

3. B. H. Roberts, *A Scrap Book*, vol. 2 (Provo, UT: Pulsipher, 1989), 101, 103.

4. Joseph Smith, *Teachings of the Prophet Joseph Smith*, comp. by Joseph Fielding Smith (Salt Lake City: Deseret, 1961), 345–47.

5. Joseph Fielding Smith, *Doctrines of Salvation*, comp. by Bruce R. McConkie (Salt Lake City: Bookcraft, 1954), 1:10.

6. Smith, *Teachings of the Prophet*, 345–47.

7. Orson Hyde, "Man to Lead God's People, etc.," in *Journal of Discourses*, vol. 1, ed. G. D. Watt (Liverpool: F. D. and S. W. Richards, 1854), 123.

8. Eliza R. Snow, *Biography and Family Record of Lorenzo Snow* (Salt Lake City: Deseret, 1884), 9–10, quoted in Gerald N. Lund, "I Have a Question," *The Ensign* (February 1982): 39.

9. Bruce McConkie, *Mormon Doctrine* (Salt Lake City: Bookcraft, 1966), 576–77.

10. Orson Pratt, "The Pre-existence of Man," *The Seer* 1, no. 3 (1853): 37.

11. Smith, *Teachings of the Prophet*, 370.

CHAPTER THREE

1. Bruce R. McConkie, *What Mormons Think of Christ* (Salt Lake City: The Church of Jesus Christ of Latter-day Saints, 1982), 22.

2. McConkie, *What Mormons Think of Christ*, 19, emphasis added.

3. Pratt, "The Pre-existence of Man," 39.

4. *Uniform System for Teaching Families* (Salt Lake City: The Church of Jesus Christ of Latter-day Saints, 1981), 15, 17, emphasis added.

5. "Teaching the Gospel," 113.

6. McConkie, *Mormon Doctrine*, 784.

7. McConkie, *Mormon Doctrine*, 778.

8. For a more detailed description of the three kingdoms, see section 76 of *The Doctrine and Covenants*.

9. John Morgan, *Plan of Salvation* (Salt Lake City: The Church of Jesus Christ of Latter-day Saints, 1978), 25.

10. McConkie, *Mormon Doctrine*, 755.

11. McConkie, *What Mormons Think of Christ*, 18–19.

12. McConkie, *What Mormons Think of Christ*, 20.

13. *Articles of Faith*, 2nd ed. (Salt Lake City: Deseret, 1901), 120.

14. Elder E. F. Perry in the *Scrap Book*, 1989.

15. Morgan, *Plan of Salvation*, 6.

CHAPTER FOUR

1. *An Address to All Believers in Christ* (Richmond, MO: David Whitmer, 1887), 64, quoted in Jerald and Sandra Tanner, *Mormonism—Shadow or Reality* (Salt Lake City: Utah Lighthouse Ministry, 1972), 179.

2. *Uniform System for Teaching Families* (Salt Lake City: The Church of Jesus Christ of Latter-day Saints, 1981), 64.

3. *Doctrine and Covenants*, 294.

4. John Widtsoe, *Priesthood and Church Government* (Salt Lake City: Deseret, 1954), 25.

5. *Uniform System*, 32.

6. *Uniform System*, 23.

7. See John Widtsoe, *Priesthood and Church Government* (Salt Lake City: Deseret, 1954), for a detailed study of the Mormon priesthood. See also Jerald Tanner, *Mormonism* (Salt Lake City: J. Tanner, 1961), especially chapter 15, for a critique of the Mormon priesthood.

CHAPTER FIVE

1. Fawn M. Brodie, *No Man Knows My History* (New York: Alfred A. Knopf, 1971), 67.

2. Sheler and Wagner, "Latter-day Struggles," 77.

3. John Ankerberg and John Weldon, *Cult Watch* (Eugene, OR: Harvest House, 1991), 37.

4. Ankerberg and Weldon, *Cult Watch*, 38.

5. Tanner, *Mormonism—Shadow or Reality*, 52.

6. For a critical study of the origins of the Book of Mormon, see Wayne L. Cowdrey, Howard A. Davis, and Arthur Vanick, *Who Really Wrote the Book of Mormon? The Spalding Enigma* (St. Louis: Concordia, 2005).

7. Tanner, *Mormonism—Shadow or Reality*, 66–67.

8. Brodie, *No Man Knows My History*, 69.

CHAPTER SIX

1. For more information, see Carlos E. Asay, "The Temple Garment: 'An Outward Expression of an Inward Commitment,'" *Liahona* (September 1999): 33–40.

2. *Uniform System*, 42.

APPENDIX A

1. *The Pearl of Great Price* (Salt Lake City: Deseret, 1981).